in early light

in early light
aubades

ISBN 9781763825994

Front cover image : Kit Kelen
Back cover image : Carol Archer

Walleah Press
South Launceston
Tasmania, Australia 7249

www.walleahpress.com.au
ralph.wessman@walleahpress.com.au

in early light

aubades

Kit Kelen

Contents

as from a dream risen

it's a somewhere sun
to trick up the hills
to show us from

a look-in

already among leaves to wing
climb beakful
get up dizzy

forgetting what came before

here's the light that breaks down doors

must be own haruspex

come blank to
early light

something, somewhere, someone's gone

as if the eyes were otherwise
knowing what's to be done

guess the bones
unravel guts

tell me which way the world

divine by them
how the day's to come

my head turns to stone

and I sleep like a forest

am woken with invented birds

the wheel of blue becoming over
all this to be alone

now the rooster
who resembles his dreams
bends down
for the first
lit worm

this parting at first light

overture

times wonder
how the daybrink dark
edges every sign for itself
with first thing singing
head of sleep

dawn's no chorus
but

good morning always
where I am

first ever

from this lit skin

looking out

as if the track
stretched on to say

sun shone to show
take care

how it will come from nothing

first light's a question thrown

even mountain's saluting the sun

we scratch
day to be of sky

to be just where this happens

the creek begins again

a roar of where it always was

a cast of light

day in parts
to assemble

pond up to a proper height

and heavens?
they're aimed in our general direction

a roar in treetops too

ontogenesis

you can almost see
one life in another

the kitchen cupboards from the floor

along a corridor
some doorway
the backdoor

round the corner, laundry
the mulberry, the washing line

you can almost reach back

on the table cigarettes too high

you've left the keycard
can't remember the room

Green Capstans

one thought overtakes another
the place has become a maze

now in the cradling arms of almost

when little enough to be held as such

veranda view
the bay blue
the up and

weed wash close
the rubbish

what was it on my plate?

almost as if you know
all of the selves before

you could invent the alphabet
to spell out the words
to call a name

up too close
taste the fire
drum of it rusted

the rhyme remembers us

the who and where we

you can almost count
almost tell the time

can you imagine?

you'll come to a mirror
who's there?

would you know where to begin?

before all this our wilderness

ways lost
dreamt to forget

the careful paws of night survived

the firstliness of birds
born to the thin air chase

cloth biplane wings of the skeleton shown
insect golden in the glint
dip, turn and gone

here's who how thus

a gong of bright
round as the day's to grow

call all wonderment
first watch

as a dog shakes pond
so sleep

my curl of claws
lost love

we never went back
we went on

Nagykaroly / Carei
one quarter of my family

these whom I never knew

and of whom so little is known
a list of names is all

something in the newspaper
a wedding, some munificence

absent the map now

names changed

one quarter of the past of me

the horse trade, a broad brim

so much beard, so little told

but how they were tricked away from time

these hearts hushed against a hope
that neighbours might yet decently

this is how far

not here but from here

all this breath gone before mine

what can I say for them?

they bury the name of the town

I must make a face in my mind
for those I never saw

imagine a queue of them leaving the world

I tell a parable standing for truth

it's when there is no one left to tell
to be told, to do the telling

so it comes to what can't be remembered

forget and go on is how it goes
is how we've lived to here

it's all against forgetting hearts set

it's how the world slips off

we are still escaping the fate
of everyone before

all the people in the dream are me

are skins of a wish

the clamour crowds of need
a pocket full of me is all

some under
some up

many just fresh fled
spill the beans

a soak into the page
still sinking

seasons beyond

there are turns
none to guess

believe every word

the leaf puts out

you feel the full force

forget about daylight
debts and loans

even the moon forgets

all the people in the dream are me

I have to mourn them gone

in the steppes
with Borodin

a conch calls
was the sea once

on horseback then
a bamboo tune

everything gathered
to keep us

it's out of the night
they came

days to a lake
no one chose this diet

life was far already
star so ringing as the dawn

last snows track
from the desert to more

a mount is pointed
tomorrow's all the destination

hooves know the way
we forget

expect a certain street to be there

imagine myself gone

face in every direction

a slatted shine
corner from which nearly

for some it is not a matter to cling

it's only now and away, nothing then

no trespass

as if on my own wings

yet one might remain

the weather fell upon

these are the traces you see

this is my page of the mirror

it's when I was far asleep
it's when I was away

beside a self

as thing is I

doesn't matter the shape

a stone inscribes a circle

as it is with everything around

there's forage
bless up on

day sudden with each thing beside

in the pages of which I am author

I could tell round
the favour returning

I am their looking glass

only now see myself

ahead, behind

we'll often take the sun for a sign
show other marks

world – stone to turn

struck day spreads out
from where

this breeze a rough guess
in the tangle
in the twinkle too

the stone is a sea
takes breath

from pebble, from grain grown

self's in what's fallen
afoot

most of the world is above one
neither far nor long
neither still

it's round as the seeing eye

we are beginning to be

the practice of less is just where we are
Kawayu Onsen, Otogawa, Wakayama

a leaf downstream

see just what
feel, touch
taste the day

are you to notice
a river makes mist of light first?

look up out
vanish cloud

no heretofore
but here and now

in order to look
you must see

it's just these little prints I leave
barest of impressions

least of it falls
through these leaves
to the floor

sometimes you won't believe where you are

so little one need bear in mind

some days a head is empty

at times hard to just be

yet water falls over a stone
one wouldn't say again
but still

you'd need to be awake to it
but, if not, it still goes

they say that in order to see
you must look

where the river is swimming
sit fish
you have to believe in them though

the practice of just where we are
is much less
than many have made it to be

one comes from the dream

as if from halls
veranda ranged
from doors forgotten to paint

wings woken
and the lilt
as through a curtain skip

the same old trick required
a climb out of mirrors
just here
to find ourselves in
this ancient glow
come where we've not
been before

first light

was a Sunday shone

the curtain cracks
moon motes spun

gentle with the all seen
everything yet to be said

was round as a pancake
sweet as jam

what was this?
and
why are we?

the legs of the track
take on

first light held
a wizard's sword
in aura

here were galoshes
shining past mud

treetops gathering to breeze
abrupt with the forms

with the lines
melted like butter away

from which we would loosen the hours

there weren't the words back then

it was always that we'd get a job
grow up, decide
keep faith like cockerspaniel
a King Charles

call it fate
to forget all these questions

we were always bound to forget ourselves
how the world was once first lit

mock orange whiff lifted
sunflower heads bowed
the left-out barrow, full of rain

often there'll be a disappearance

you'll wait till you can't remember

I was looking for you

I'm carrying the still wet canvas

now and then I'd work
even as it drips

another country
winter still
still early

so searching
but no utterance

no wallet
no pass

was led
as far as
I forgot

later, who?
where were you?

what a fool I'd been
day just coming on

you will rise with this

then all of it is true

we, the imagineers

prisoners

see into the melody
out of the fog

under a veil of holies

I call it a life away
tell a thing gone

show my new passport
to another door

wake from
so many, so much

a question
thrown
over all

night train to Vatra Dornei
in Bukovina

much of it is village dimly
coup upon coup
cropping through flat lands

hear only the speech of steel wheels
track clatter and rattle, all to the north

towers of old smoke until the mountains come

passing away like a country, the night
the place that was before

in through an open window, it is a headlong thing

the Romans laid these Dacia lines
this must be the thousand year train

undoze for first gleam

fine cloud, coarse
barns to fill, hummocks ring

peach, birch, pine

a mess of wires, cranes, river runs
all the industrial trackside leavings

and from some windows
clothes hung to freeze

old car wrecks cast to the sidings
churchyards full of the gone

the stolid station master with the flag
now all the flush tints come

mist yet here there too

the valley opening, opening
whole farms dance

the green all greener than the hill is high

fences and tracks leading where

tin tile timber roof
crosses all round

old walls and yellow wells
the road itself runs by

snow pockets the furthest view

wet grass, my dewed legs
webs shone through
whose is this dripping leaf?

in someone's reverie

dark woods

chorded as these colours are

there's weather in the head

its own world spinning

where I am furled

and bells ring there

a sapling springs

some say
like a heart
pumped round

then the pinking
to unfold

a path in the garden
where day is home

a firstness edged
all wings attend

up flutter, find
and say

must be our spark

there's no one here in charge
no one to thank or blame

keep to the fire

like a sign from dreamdeeps
and then one more

the ant trail

there's falling
there's coming round
sitting up
to clench
to stim

full of wings, the stillness
a song tells on

the turn too slow to see
but blink

it grows to the eye
alas

words from another place are here

in a comfortable chair by which

keep the fire
look in

even the moment spreads out as a ripple

you may think
it's wrong of the dead to be gone

glow grows

paws of the dark attend

cling in our raft of each to each

still to the point of touch
or that's how it looks from here

even this G-type yellow dwarf comes up

there's a trick of the heart to go on

sometimes waking wonder why

this skin
and pulse of ache

how the dark is edged

a funny shape
appendaged

this world turns out
mind of its own

how light will come from nothing

we've just met those
who meant so much

echoes fading now

rub back a primed sky to find

pillow for head upon

so many tribes of birds
at it and gone

ways overgrown
and chase some insect
unknown make

it's every day for a first

the music to which I aspire

start off on the track but it's already there

should it ever come to intentions

a sun is shone to show

little wing bursts
of a wren took off
first blue after rain

first thing is singing

the day to be of what's here

go up in it, just like that

first thing singing

someone is coming out of the soil
someone goes further down

stand back for the sense of it
look sideways

there's so much can't be helped

one bird bluer than the rest
away

it is of course a day of the week

there's how we, for instance

wake up to this
wake up to yourself

think of it all as given
if you think of it at all

little bird come

full of what's
neither speech
nor song

come
to the other world's window
to wish

namelessly
and I know you

little bird
do you think
I am mirrored in this?

mine is the pond stood up
nothing bends beak

a hit! see so much
in the rain's round soul

all your angles, calculation
heights, swoop
resistances of air

for love, for a meal, for a drink

how alien inward I am
to your trajectory

no branch, no twig
sufficient
but to the tip

instinct to work
so play this way

and curious
landed, peer
nested

come to the window to wish
as insect otherworldly

in the stilled wind

not a scratch of this up

your sun is

you are teaching me
may I guess?

just this?
what mystery to each
we others always are

little bird gone
let's say
you are much missed

socks damp through
with the dawn excursion
gumboots know a hole

arrive

good morning always
where I am

head full of still

a way to go

as if the track
stretched out a hand
so as to say

you must be the original here

first ever

in this skin
all lit

just the one shot
at this day

it's every wake up

to forgive

thread of light
a mist might wear

so it is day
and words appear

this chatter not a choir

a touch

as if that were why we are lit again
as if that were why we are here

let the creatures come

let them lap at
browse till wander

still the open hand of a wish

stand in my socks to welcome
have their saying to heart
feather as we go

all their griefs piled
decorous

crawl out of what
drop down
buzz in

they rise from out of
words must fail

it's here about my business go

to trust the creatures come

fine mist

through which sun shows branches

birds hidden in their song

frog knock

first up
scratch into yellow

a certain stretch familiar

dew falling yet

though burrow some
eyes paint first

make day
it's healing over me

where the waters reflect

the screen I'll outstare is the sky

in fine fog

you could be anywhere home
wait for glint
no wind but otherworldly

expect lost cities, gorgeous towers

sometimes from the lifting

days waiting in a sunshine fold

were we not always witnessing?

a river then the sudden blue

and other colours come

lines fray through

wool over
in a winter mist

sometimes stars
shone like leaves from rain

they will be hidden
all are

one wonders where a page will spill

sometimes a daylit moon too full

all this ushering in

and you yourself a door

take treetops in a fresh lit pond

nor landing but skim by

come in come out of
under standing
how it is, was, will
to be away nowhere and be here just

there's no elsewhere quite like this
there isn't another planet of it

go into the mist
and be mossed

sometimes looking out of it
take care
to be just where we happen

failed dawn

remember Mayakovski

night has levied a tax of stars in the sky

I write to you, o planet
wonder how to say it all

the various conditions
objective, otherwise

resistances
taste of water
the great historic sleeps

I wish to murder everyone
but it passes, don't worry

hold a knife to my own throat

hell's, after all, a self
there's no need of others

we are unnatural disasters

the level field
where we have fallen
the forest griefs
would not have guessed

no one sees me as high risk

fire inside
a little engine I

you won't know what's a plea

go back!
go back!

one little pill
what a difference

fingers scattered, broken
the love boat all cracked up

on blue disc

time is weather

clouds all the great events
in life and world historic –
birthdays, revolutions

all of the bringing to light
still up there
for all to see

each thing spoken
goes around
curses, blessings
prophecies float by

on that world
after an all nighter
any dawn

it's never the same sun rises
every god gets a turn

everyone sees what was
may be

it helps to think
things are

day's naked
we're our own pyjamas

dance around for an hour at dawn
just to see what's up

on such a planet
silly with the wind
we're like kids in a classroom
want out

but that was never

a slow drip sky
waking to weather

early in the afternight

grey
then one must lamp it

all blear
becalmed
a stumble is

green therefrom
as dim

no timpani

breeze to top
in the leaves

in tree beneath
the afterfalls

nothing sharp
not a line

there were no
splendid rays

you wouldn't think there'd ever been stars
not even a sliver moon

day brink

a little agony

here was a royal road

map imagined

a run at the creek
it lifts me

love left us with a cardboard sign
direction no longer remembered

but we went

radiant as the very idea

daylight dissolves our means

far from the song on wings
day spreading
and we are so far

time to the other place
where it's we are passing now

not so cold as it should be

each in own steam

sheds and a truck shudder passing

many gleam

so much tin
we could open a sky

green in the drought
sunlight ours

a persistence

from out of weather
a wisp
and winter curlicue

heaven to a cloud

various blossoms begin

the sphere is tipping again
and faster than anyone flies
this spin

mulberry's out trapping sun
various blossoms begin
the cherry and the peach, much crocus
jonquil already and everywhere wattle

so many nameless
and some called weed

from the trod, the fallen
out of the compost
first sly salutes
mulch makes its way of life

rose rise
push petals round
they scent the shop

let's not name the season yet

it's all sung for
and some will laugh

some to seed
the coriander!

now the branches
breakfast decked
feathers attend

a lily rise
some trumpet too

fanfare
all for love
the drawing in
showers and

plaintive yet
to a regret

implicated in such hearts
these shapes!
the gone of the dark that was!

no one could dream them up

did anyone see the bud come?
who was it first unfurled?
pumpkin sits for its bright

who worships whom is hard to say
or can we catch this conversation?

come all ye insects, dance now
we take this sphere so much as read

it takes us for a spin

how often far with

out of time

tether ending till
we're left

brittle, thrilled with
run to dust

motion's lack unsaid
tune seeping
from on high

slept as far as
dreamt until
bright spires

licked
still tiptoe wits

town in the all abandoned

dream and you're there
there's no delay

dawn parts the heart

day lapping at these paws

call it laughter
this warding away
kookaburra borders

seed

we cling
a little wrestle up
wilderness thereof

left

a little of the nightmare weight

the present present to us too

heart head parting
line unseen

tiny corner I call

there's no such person
never will be, was

even a mountain's addressing the sun

first light's a question thrown

just a little colour shows

a rusted hammer for the dawn

the perfect shapes of sleep

open your eyes

it's all world
nowhere but

however brief

a stretch to reach

the march of stars

times fold a phrase in
or say
salute

it's with the gone
all must remain

duty bids us on

in all directions, day

have you seen?
how large a part of me it is

other worlds touch too

with all that's seared into our sight

what instinct bid

possessed of many and so much

at strings, at colour, at the keys

a room full of trees
air all eyes
all in

a page shown through
the gorgeous far

where night surrounds
our animal ends

somewhere there's a star explodes
cruel the wars and woes

it stretches out before
it shrinks

I am involved in this

in every bright where

All you did was wreck my bed, and in the morning, kick me in the head
— Rod Stewart and Martin Quittenton

time now
so you and I
must else

or otherwise
by whims of why

beyond itself
for fire our far
and only rose to tend

this pink in breeze
bed's edge unseen

a looming list
of light
day till

made season of
all sang

not yet
not yet

but each
in other's arms up

how you were tucked into

lovely and cosy and nook

who knew?
why…
only
you and I

dawn is hardly a chorus

the works begin
with raising a sun

no one knows whose

often from pond or sea

so raucous!
each commands the others

and so the universe invents
(passive voice)
flickering wings of the first tree

then lemons take to their branches for light

webs of never

none can guess what's next

it's just where I am unseen
dawn's yet feathered to sing

wandering off in the big book

by joy of self
a leaf to mark
day set down

with my own machinery
ladders and not-quite-lawns

where someone was digging
a wallaby where

wink, rotate the ears
note this
a very traipse
a hop off home

make the open
with our eyes

some several acres let

and over the tinkle hills too

dell at my disposal

a welcome to my breeze beyond

wandering off
where you'll find me
to this moment

the book's in my head
on the way

the truth (yet again)

the truth long lost
and it shines
like a dew spangled flag
dawn sets alight

I salute it
and sing it
stand like the rest
I bow for it

at times I believe
it is the truth deceived us
so simple a thing
we must have imagined

then must I not set
such doubts aside?

truth is I am here to tell
as others before

old initials
are carved in a wall

the moss grows over
the lichen speaks

truth we scratch at
dig down for

I'm a fool for it
like destiny

salute it
and sing it
stand like the rest
and I bow low

before
bow after

there must be a garden
of this truth to tell

they say the future
will bear all out

I see my horizon approach

lightning strikes to light the way

I believe the truth's a lost longing
dawn sets alight
and it shines like

a dew spangled flag
I salute it and sing it
and bow like the rest

any old animal does

me-rise

and first bright
none tending towards

there's day brain
from under covers
like a cold edge creep

thing to another
where I have been

catch faster than fire
the hidden of heart

birdsong core of light to keep

a stoking —
trick of here, sleight of how
where have we been?

in the other language
where I'm corrected
travel back
on night's lit fuse

pile image
toss inkling at

unword the wish for home

but none of this is the shining that was
that kept the spread up branches
until some shadow grows

a road was always there

umpteenth

the firstness was a garden'
sprinkled dust of star, a spell

you'll recognize
it's lit, still kissed

some trumpet for a date, a time

as for the firstness
I think it has a stale shoes smell
as of another age
or planetisimal

rain so far as it fell

lasts till we dissolve in it

then the leaves come all alight
so see how far we are

a sky is always beginning

waking, one looks for it

in my head till now

wherever you look up

there all night long
now gone

some heavenly body
just beside

all glory in the aftershine

when even a cloud appears

make my steps smaller

for the Gore Cove Track Series

and the day will stretch

over stump stone
twig till

come treetops trill
rouse breath

go on

nothing said
but the wattle up

picture as you go
be less
to see

upward tangle
rockface seeping

just by puddle
mirror this

engine block
with turkey vanish

listen for the creek beside

come from a blur
to focus

tide's out
I'm along

get it all down
soon gone

so many suns rising

a black and a white and between
much missed
by night or cloud came

not like Donne's
aloof, rule bound
careless of time

one I'll have for my back later on
and then a shielding sun
low, coming home

it's out of the sea or a mountain
it's all along the creek and fronding

some say yesterday the same
some predict tomorrow

and there are fools claim there's just one
when so many suns are rising

little Ode to Aten

and over the Koolonock Range it comes
through treetops at winter angle

I owe this one a salute

so find the limbs to offer
but mainly just admire
shade hazing
as an aura spread

the glistener
of pond tops, leaves
and solitary swagger trees
cast golden in their paddock round

the blinding casts my shadow
and every shadow else must show
how singularly small we are
who crawl this well lit Earth

how to live in a house
arriving at Soaring Gardens
a thanks to Ora Lerman

little windows of the first bright

it gathers me
from glint to blinding

like light from where
the summer mow

a window fog glassiness

deer first thing framed
old apple fall

the squirrel runup then

here's a trick
though not so on the other side where

even when gone
kitchen meadow's lit

road runs by
more often not

which people
kind safe
for their why
and other us

in one I wish and sit for fall
I mean for the turning beyond of

it's endless the bright close sprawl ideas

out of a country of conquest, gun
misery also brought

violence ever about to begin
to go on

the gone with us here enable
a call to conversation

and need to paint it
from the outside in

in the jungle of just where we happen
vale my friend, Gina Ghioni

in the music of rain
a bright patch
where we saw the whales

you'd love the light here
a flutter
squirrel up
first shadows
forest thereof
hills rolling away

moments like this
I go into a poem
where
you are the roof and the walls
and the style

you know
this is what I do

dear friend, you're with me
here now
almost autumn
the leaves though still

all green as far as the eye

now the sun comes up
without itself

the rest of us left bereft
go on with the ache of you gone

anonymous ocean

jetlag series

the koel and your snore –
a syncopation

it's at such a time you hear the whole world

losing a day mid Pacific
making week without a Wednesday

having lost the words that came
now parted from

lying down for all the correct hours

calculating time everywhere

in the healing deeps of

gently in the now until

that's how we're getting there

the day after forever
a world to end it all

shops are open again

unexpectedly we're all still here

it's a blue moon Sunday month in Bush Week

you have to sing for it
believe!

this is a question

and here we are again
it's all shone so

we're monkeys again
and we're ants

it's everyone on a way for themselves
it's all of us together

here we go
butting up the back cover

have to imagine our own ending

life is larger now

in beetle bright, in the vanish
Kumano Kodo

a morning shines

the way's just these steps

hatless, as day begins

or a frog gets out of the way

one will slow to the pace of the trail

even here I could call Pitt St
and bright the haze away

here's the rhythm of it
I'm a ghost too

there are times you'll think you've written a line
but the line is waiting still

there's looking back
and see you've gone

a bend in time

those footsteps behind, my own

they say you'd hear the stillness
but for what's still in your head

and then the moon's our sun

ekphrastic for Frederic Leighton's 1884 'Cymon and Iphigenia'

soul's up
hound attends

after abandon
Bacchic languor
the dream deeps of the day

and lost in these folds
oakspread
under laurel, under bay

robed round with a table cloth

it's ticklish under there

no one knows where to find this sea

woke up one morning

Lieber Herr Gott, mach mich stumm, Das ich nicht nach Dachau komm
– popular 1935 jingle

I'll never mix carrot juice and radish juice again
– Bugs

and the underug was out, was gone

how's that?
what's up?
who? where?

'surely it's not?'
you'll hear those whispers

the voice less, less

it's fascism 101

call them what you are
accuse
that's crazy
there'll be no more elections

call your lie this truth

call them ugly

they don't know

the system, even broken goes into its old routines

in this case, that's blame

soft shoe, slapstick
a funny thing happened…

but it's not anymore

it was a long time back and salute
remember who we were

that wasn't us at all

 let's all play pretend
do dizzies too

close your eyes till it's safe again

there's a fire
they're coming for us

the voice is going

this is the path
from broken to gone

we polish the teeth of the wheel
where the ship is going down

it takes imagination

the chug chug of machine

grinding of other bones

it's trying to turn things
it's stuck

but one goes with the fantasy

they won't know who they are

things are okay
we'll all be alright

aren't we better off already?

phew! that was a close call

this is the same place after all

but it's not
and we're not
it never was
we won't be ever again

all time is catastrophic

in the field between of stars

you're out making distance
receding

all of a type
lit distantly

say these things to yourself

how it's better than real to be

just as gone as good

in just our underwords

and under them are always more

these other moments, lives
just as we see
each infinite
nor thought

and if, by chance
this world is curved
we'll ride it round
face foes
trip wires

we'll go so far
as never know
there can't be a way back

it was time had me

off on adventures
prone to foretell

a curious delve
and made it my bible

kept a life there

and time is death as well
trumpet edged
round as the coin to drop
come the day

a strange notation
clockwise

roll it out
like a rug
like the tongue
a sea shoring

come closer
told timber in the rings
come kiss

nothing's everlasting
everything's outlasting me

time folds like the flower to wilt
holds to its golden grip

and taken by the blue
eyes up
sad with the very ends

one had to live as far as this
survive all selves to tell

up to catch the day

here where I've been thrown
and in the act

with both paws
all fours

beanful
up leapt into
unblear

come at it edgewise
like the bird, suspecting

you crowds I am
now lost gone

from wordless where
there'll be to flower

we have to call it
a day

in this our here and now

be woke

from the make believe
from the usual

my pride wide eyes
all the world let in

events overtake
heart raising from the dark

like to say never too late but

see everywhere the sleepers

ask yourself what will it take
to end the pretending

sudden as the sun we'll be

to act
once we are woke

it dawns on me

to look again

the future is our secret arrangement

we keep it close
tell no one

all kinds of things may be predicted but

it's quite a way to come

you've climbed peak, no guarantees

the future, too, will be everywhere
just as far as that goes

these are the ruins of what was
the true parts must lie under

though it will come
it's to distract

despite the propheteering
a future's never as foretold

efficiency is all about guilt
the need to fit what's here

take self from day – where's time?
we fail

walk with the creek, take turns
who has precedence?
who knows?

still there'll be sun shimmer
where the river's morning runs

we will – won't we? – return

night falls to it too

please tell me just that you'll be here

I write the book till it falls apart
I hope that you'll read this way

About the author

Christopher (Kit) Kelen is a poet and painter, resident on Worimi lands, in the Myall Lakes of NSW, Australia. Published widely since the seventies, he has more than a dozen full length collections in English as well as translated books of poetry in Chinese (several), Portuguese (several), French, Italian, Spanish, Indonesian, Swedish, Norwegian, Filipino, Greek, Romanian and Esperanto. Kit's latest volume of poetry in English is *Book of Mother*, published by Puncher & Wattmann in 2022. Kit has shortlisted for and won poetry prizes since the eighties (an ABC/ Bicentennial Award). His first book *The Naming of the Harbour & the Trees* won an Anne Elder in the nineties. In 2017, Kit was shortlisted twice for the Montreal Poetry Prize and won the Local Award in the Newcastle Poetry Prize. In 2019 and 2020 Kit won the Hunter Writers' Centre award in the NPP. He was also shortlisted for the ACU prize in 2020. In 2021 he won the bronze medal in the Newcastle Poetry Prize. In 2022 he won the second prize silver medal. In 2023, he won the Hunter Writers' Centre award. In 2024 Kit Kelen was the winner of the Newcastle Poetry Prize.

Kit has been writer/artist in Residence in many parts of the world – in Australia, Italy, Sweden, Norway, Spain, Iceland, Finland, Romania, the US and Cyprus. A number of these residencies have led to book publications – for instance Bundanon Residencies produced his books *Time with the Sky* and *To the Single Man's Hut.* Time at the Messen residency on the Hardanger Fjord produced *Poor Man's Coat* and a book in Norwegian entitled *Glasfjorden* (the glass fjord). Kit has had ten solo painting and drawing exhibitions – in Australia, Portugal, Spain, Sweden and Macao. Recent exhibitions include *Palimpspectre* (in 2023, at the Manning Regional Gallery, NSW) and *word & unword* (2024) at the WORDXIMAGE gallery in Maitland.

Emeritus Professor of English at the University of Macau, where he taught for many years, Kit Kelen is also a Conjoint Professor at the University of Newcastle. Series Editor for Flying Islands Pocket Poets Series (with now more than one hundred volumes), Kit has mentored many poets and translators from various parts of the world, and run a number of on-line communities of practice in poetry (most notably Project 366 [from 2016-2020]). He currently runs Flying Islands' yearlong on-line poetry manuscript workshop. You can follow Kit's work-in-progress at *the Daily Kit* – https://thedailykitkelen.blogspot.com/